Time Signatures

Time Signatures

Poems by

John W. Bing

Cover design by Shay Culligan
Cover Photo by Isaac Ibbott
Author Photo by Carl Haag (used with Permission)

ISBN: 978-1-954353-00-8

Kelsay Books
502 South 1040 East, A-119
American Fork, Utah, 84003

To Cass, who knits it together

To my family, my dear ones

To my friends, who taught me as only friends can

Acknowledgments

The Trickster: "An Afghan Morning," "Then, Again"

Exit 13: "Tourist Trap" (Originally titled "Reading the Jungle")

Friends of Afghanistan: "The Juniper Bush," "The Wind, the Dust"

Contents

Testing Time

Family Time

Desert Time

Afghan Time

An Afghan Morning

Darkness and time
swirl in memory. What no longer exists
lives now.

The grasshoppers begin their waking buzz. Then, out of the darkness of the earliest desert dawn figures appear, walking in small groups, riding donkeys, or simply sitting with their goods. Around them are the outlines of mountains in one direction, the empty desert fading to the horizon in another. From chimneys of mud houses rise the thin smoke of early morning fires. Some sit with birds in wooden cages, waiting for a later sun to go to market. Some walk besides donkeys or camels laden with blood oranges, pomegranates, grapes, melons. In a nearby street, a turbaned figure cooks kabobs, marinated in yoghurt and garlic overnight, over a charcoal fire. Others walk toward their morning labor in the bazaars. All are silent.

Confined by
mountain and desert, set in time,
fate molds each to its place.

The Water Carrier

Ghazni, Afghanistan, winter of 1966

At the door an old man with a dirt-grey turban and a blanket
wrapped around his body carried a sheep-bladder filled with water
over his shoulder into the dark mud-walled house to fill a basin,

then, given a few small coins, departed somewhere to fill again his
burden.
I sat with new friends in full winter, eating dried fruits on a low
covered table
while underneath, a *bukhari* with hot embers kept the cold at bay.

Later, one of them brought me to a teahouse and we sat
for hours as a waiter filled our pot of tea from copper samovars,
our first cups sugared. I tasted sweetness fade to bitter at the last
cup.

Then I leaned back and saw the beauty of the cold
Hindu Kush, the long reach of mountain streams,
and smelled soot in the air from a thousand fires.

In memory, Ghazni will lie always in that winter
when pomegranates from the bazaar froze solid
and an earthquake turned the hotel chandelier

into a long pendulum swinging between my past
and my future. If I had known what was to come
I could not have done differently.

Once, a pack of dogs followed me until,
backed against a mud wall, I threw an imaginary stone
as I do now. The dogs fled.

Afghan Pantoum

Back and forth swung the chandelier
as I ate in the restaurant, alone.
A quiet waiter at my side said
Not to worry, sir, the quake will soon be done.

As I ate in the restaurant, alone,
thinking of home, thinking of the cold.
Not to worry, it will soon be done
And things will settle down, I'll be home.

Thinking of home, thinking of the cold,
in the bazaar, buying an orange frozen hard.
Things will settle down and I'll be home,
sitting in a hidden garden in Herat.

In the bazaar, buying an orange frozen hard.
Then spring came, mulberry trees in bloom.
After sitting in a hidden garden in Herat
I began to feel at home.

Then spring came, mulberry trees in bloom,
a quiet waiter brought pots of sugared tea.
I began to feel at home.
Back and forth swings the chandelier.

When Elephants Fight

"When elephants fight, the grass is trampled."
So they say in parts of Africa, where elephants have roamed
since empires began their good works. And before.

I remember. My first trip to Baghlan, through the Salang Pass,
built by the Russians, which later became the highway
for their troops and tanks. They destroyed so much

in that small country. Then the Afghans destroyed their Empire.

Our bus was mired in the blizzard near the top of the pass,
stuck in a line of trucks trying to get to the tunnel.
The windows were loose, and the wind blew through.

I remember. A soldier lent me his blanket, and asked about my
health
while other soldiers worked to free the mired bus.
Then we began to move again. We parted at a little store.

I wonder if he survived, if he remembers that foreigner, after all
the wars.

Leaving Baghlan

Way north of Kabul, among the mud houses and students,
Mohammed, Aziz, Yasin, Ali, Ehsan and thirty-five more,
here, here, here, here, present, sir.

The classes outside, a *jouie* running beside the chairs
under mulberry trees, under the sun, under the mist,
the brave boys sitting in rows, eager to learn.

Where are your parents? How much money do you have?
Why did you come here so far away from home?
Will you remember us when you have gone?

We'd been two years away from the familiar.
Now peaceful nights, moonlit, drifting, ancient,
utter quiet broken by a donkey's bray.

Earthquakes shook the house, caving in the well;
Lettuce grew in the garden. In the compound
we fattened a Thanksgiving turkey named Hubert.

The mayor, newly met, invited us
to say goodbye. We ate dinner cross-legged,
chicken hidden under mounds of rice.

Sent upstairs to find the bathroom, I found
three daughters, giggling, in their make-up and finery,
hidden my two years under their moving tents.

As a parting gift, the mayor loaned his jeep,
filled with a caged bird and eight fat-tailed sheep
and us, face to tail, leaving Baghlan.

What was to become of them, after we left,
Mohammed, Aziz, Yasin, Ali, Ehsan,
here, here, here, here, present, sir?

What was to become of us, leaving in peace, returning with guns
Jim, Steve, John, Mary, Sam,
here, here, here, here, present, sir?

The Afghan Woman, 1968

For Kris Engstrom

In the photograph, I see
a young Afghan woman who looks old,
head hooded by a shroud, staring past the camera.

In her face are the years she has lived
and the years to come. Her face, half lit,
half shadowed, is not hopeful, but resigned.

In her eyes she sees the warplanes that will fly
over her land, the soldiers that are to fight,
her children who will go hungry.

Is she Pashtun? Tadjik? Hazarrah? No one
knows, and it only matters that her fate bound her
to the mountains and deserts of her country

and to the iron laws of custom and culture
that made her a captive in the valleys
and the forgotten of the forgotten.

In this face I sense the photographer, a friend,
who offered a moment of dignity
for a woman who would have little.

In this poem I remember that friend who
valued the women she met there, who managed
to save what God abandoned, like this woman.

In the end, we prize our memories
of courage, sacrifice and strength.
They rise in history, and in us,

like clouds, like the sun, like mountains.
Now this woman, call her Leila,
is also with you.

Witnesses

She heard the rumble and the
shattering of glass.
Later she noticed her kitchen windows
blown out, that morning in

Kabul
Paris
London
Beirut
New York
Damascus
Homs
Cairo

She took water, bandages and broom,
went to the streets
began patching, mending, cleaning
blood, skin and rubble from the streets.

Meanwhile, passersby stood by
looking, whispering, taking photos for Facebook,
which would collect likes and make their friends aghast.
Watching, watching, watching, in

Cairo
Homs
Damascus
New York
Beirut
London
Paris
Kabul

Then, Again

Mohammed is the name my father gave to me.
My family name is Ibrahim.
We are from the north, near the border
and it was once peaceful.
    So it was then, so shall it be again.

Before the Khan named Ghengis it was peaceful,
we had much water for our crops,
it flowed from wells through dugouts underground
carved under the hard land.
    So it was then, so shall it be again.

Genghis and his men destroyed our wells
and the desert bloomed again—with sand.
Our crops were ruined, we were left in rags.
We will not forgive those Mongols, some still with us.
    So it was then, so shall it be again.

Then came the British with their whores
and fancy coats and guns and cooks!
One day we killed them all, almost,
as they ran to Hindustan.
    So it was then, so shall it be again.

The Russians were godless, not people of the Book,
and tried to stuff us with their ideas and beliefs,
Corrupting the young, spitting on the Quran;
We sent them packing and destroyed their empire.
    So it was then, so shall it be again.

Then came the Americans. They fought the Talibs,
down south, who had protected Saudis as their guests.
They stirred up trouble, here and in America.
For a while things settled down, it seemed.
    So it was then, so shall it be again.

But the foreigners came back to fight again.
They told us how to vote and to disrobe the women.
And so many fought them. What would you have done?
We are from the North, and it was once peaceful.
    So it was then, so shall it be again.

Mohammed is the name my father gave to me.
My family name is Ibrahim. In my son's time, or his son's,
it will be peaceful again. And, Insha'Allah, water will flow
from deep underground, to nourish and sustain.
    So it was then, so shall it be again.

The Wind, the Dust

In Memoriam, Mohammed Ehsan Entezar

The day is hot, and a dry wind blows.

I stand with many men
in three lines facing the bier.
The mullah's cloak flutters in the wind.
After instructions, we stand together
in silent prayer. The men make a bowl
with their hands. Then the body
of my old friend is carried by the men
to the deep grave. The mullah
asks for three men from the family
to descend to the grave
to receive the body.

Dust blows in the hot wind around the grave.

Three men drop into the opening. The mullah
instructs them to receive the body,
how to lay the body down facing Kaaba.
The men lift the body, wrapped
in a white kaftan, from the bier,
gently place it in the proper position.
They are pulled out. The mullah
and one of the family speak surahs from the Quran.
The mullah turns to us and says
there is a grave for each of us,
it awaits us.

                He instructs the three
to throw dust into the grave. They beckon me
to follow and I take a handful of dust.
I throw it to my friend

and the wind throws it back to me.

Near the Borders

After Frida Kahlo's "Self Portrait Near the Border between Mexico and the United States of America," 1932

The border between sun and moon
The border between smoke and the flag
The border between temples and skyscrapers
The border between idols and factories
The border between *campo* and industry
The border between sanity and madness
The border between sleep and sight
The border between he and she
The border between us and them
The border between love and hate
The border between black and white
The border between police and the people
The border between the wealthy and the rest
The border between truth and lies
The border between danger and safety
The border between war and peace
The border between history and magic
The border between Mexico and the U.S.
The border near the wall

Everyone lives near the border,
Especially those who believe they live safely
    on the right side.

Mashacket Cove

There lies his white sailboat,
rudder raised, mast down,
sail furled, near the water
on a patch of green salt marsh.

The keel has dug into the earth
and rust scars the paint,
No wind moves this boat
From its earthen mooring.

No birds, no other boats,
just waves which, stopped,
wait forever to gently
break on shore.

Up from the white sailboat,
at the limit of sight,
the eye finds a white strip of beach
where the Great Pond and ocean meet.

Nighthawks

*The **common nighthawk** is a medium-sized crepuscular or nocturnal bird*

I'm after ME.—Edward Hopper

The night is pierced with shafts
of yellow light shining up at tenements
from curving café windows.

Inside the diner
three figures sit holding mugs or a glass.
Two wear the same fedora.

The men look to be the same
man, one from the back
one from the front, the same fedora.

The woman examines a book of matches
with which a man's cigarette has just
been lit, one of the men with the fedora.

The one with his back to the glass is Hopper.
The fourth figure hunches in front of massive
urns washing dishes hidden from view.

The counter is almost bare.
Almost nothing is there.
This is nowhere.

They have been there all night.
They will be there forever.
The café has no exit.

Tourist Trap

The howlers begin their rumbling chant.

The jungle holds no mysteries to those
who can name each tree,
each leaf, each feathered movement
in the green hidden undergrowth.
They see in a leaf, in the bark,
a potion, a passion, a cure, a history
of their people. They know the blue-tailed
dragonfly brings good luck,
the wild Cashew Tree's fruit will poison
if not first roasted, that branches of the Pochote Tree
when planted closely make a living fence,
that leaves of the Panama tree make a healing tea.

Visitors come to see the Mot-Mot, the Elegant Trogon
or the Blue-Throated Golden Tail hummingbird,
not the plain Clay-Colored Robin.
But those who work the fields know
the robin sings just before
the season of rain arrives, to release them
from the time of dryness and let the
planting begin.

But for those who know no names,
who walk blindly through the forest,
those who talk idly of their last night of mojitos,
and look through the scopes at feathered colors
they never saw before, or will see again—
when the guide speaks of snakes and poisonous insects,
and to beware the Pochote's sharp spines
or they hear the Howler Monkeys—they run
for home and their favorite wilderness TV show.

Natural Order

Your then was not my then
and your now is not even my now.

Anonymous source for Our Kids: The American Dream in Crisis (Robert Putnam)

I

Rosie disappeared
Howdy Doody appeared
We all dangled.

Men wore ties
Women wore skirts
Boys combed hair
Girls had bangs
Cars had fins
Vets had college,
Gave them wings.

Father knew best
Mothers were mothers
Children grew
God was in his heaven
We were in the suburbs
We were in the ghetto
The circus was stately
We were all perfect
Arranged just so.

II

Sexual Intercourse began
Clouds appeared
Missiles in Cuba
Marilyn died
JFK shot
Then Martin and Bobby
Sit-ins
Boys to Vietnam
Fathers got drunk
Mothers awoke to
Kent State, the shots rang out
In Cambodia, Laos, all over Indochina
Thousands came to the Pentagon
Drugs, divorce, wars
Politician whores
Crosses burned
One two three four
We don't want your fucking war.

III

Women emerged from their cocoons,
Warriors, fighting
For lives in families
That no longer understood them.

Your then was not my then.

Rooms Where Nothing Happens

"I've been waiting four hours,"
said the woman with long, stringy hair

holding the crying boy
so carefully in her arms.

A man came in clutching his arm,
wearing a backwards cap and camouflage.

While the chairs filled,
one nurse, tired, worked on triage.

An old lady came in with her son,
twenty-five, maybe. He was quietly cursing.

A young woman, nursing her child,
looked both desperate and sad.

The form asked for insurance. Address.
Names. Bank accounts. Insurance?

Meanwhile, in another room where not much happens,
the men on TV, who had insurance, talked about those without.

No one in the first waiting room
paid any mind. They knew better.

Moving On or Entropy

"Time naturally flows in a way that increases disorder."
—Physics Text on the second law of thermodynamics

Everyday things disappear at the end of the line.
Scattered boxes—nothing seems to stay,
here at the beginning and the end of time.

Where's my shirt, my favorite hat, the fine
moon that glimmers even in the day?
Everyday things disappear at the end of the line.

The black rhino, the ibex, lost in the slime,
shot down, disappearing into the grey,
here at the beginning of the end of time.

The fires that blacken and cinder the oak and pine,
and the floods that turn our city streets to clay,
every day things disappear at the end of the line.

Even your voice, rich as vintage wine,
its beauty, echoing away, it couldn't stay
here at the beginning of the end of time.

And *you* and *you,* the loves that chime
Have begun to vanish along the way.
Every day things disappear at the end of the line,
Here at the beginning of the end of time.

Just a Child of the Gods

In Breugel's painting of the fall of Icarus,
only his leg appears above the green waters.
No one notices the boy, not even the fisherman
casting his line into the Icarean Sea.

No one cared. He was simply not a celebrity.
Had he been a star of mythology, with good
ratings, imagine the crowds lining the shore
as he flapped his wings and made his escape.

Imagine the cheers and applause as he leapt
into the sky, as he flew over the waters,
an ancient Evel Knievel to the adoring crowds.
Some might have imagined a romantic future

with the lovely boy, of sharing a flight or two.
If only he had not flown too close to the sun
and melted his soft wax wings. After, his fans
would have thrown flowers into the sea.

But no one noticed. Except for us. For us, he is hubris.
Only we, the myriads over the centuries, paint him
not as a hero, not as a star (which he never reached)
but, like us, a child of the gods who failed.

The Attic Owl

"The Owl of Minerva spreads its wings only at dusk." —Hegel

The cold winter sun abandons the field
to half-light, then dusk, and at the edge
eyes swivel in a feathered neck and steal

quick glances at an outlined hedge.
Beyond there lies the distant view
of two armies that fight with spear and wedge.

Ancient enemies, Athens and Sparta hew
to their essences of art and war.
These two fight on in me and you.

Each of us battles at our core
with those oppositions that at last
reveal in us the less, and the more.

Be it wisdom, or death, by the breath of wings,
till the owl flies, we know not what it brings.

The Search for Meaning

A Golden Shovel (after William Carlos Williams)

It is difficult
to get the news from poems
yet men die miserably every day
for lack
of what is found there.

Too much news: we can't find it.
The ground is over-crowded, the light is
bad, each decade is more difficult.

Soon it will be too late to
find out right from wrong, to get
past the shouting from the screens, the
blues that comes in with the news—
so what are we to take from
poems?

                Rhyme, meter, essence, of course, yet
something more, perhaps, that men,
women, children, can learn, so not to die,
not to live miserably
in bondage to every
cloud-filled, rain-burdened day.

What are they looking for?
What do they lack?

Do this: Turn off the news. Let's speak of
tenderness, of caring, that is what
we miss, that is
what is to be found,
not here, but somewhere in poems, *there.*

The Round

The last light from the west fades.
The little wind is cold, a prologue to
the darkened shiver and sheen of winter,
moving the shadowed limbs in dumb show
of frightened hands against the night.

In the fall, evening is the quiet time,
the wind softer than winter's loud drafts,
which bring the hush of white only after howling night.

Spring has the gentle sounds of wind-chimes
and the cacophony of birdsong, each species
speaking only to itself,

while summer beats like a drum, heating the blood
with radiant suns and growth of green and then,
toward the end, harvests sun-fed reds and greens,
consumed in noisy bacchanalia.

But now, all that is past. The failing light
dims the seasons, ends the round.
The ground grows hard; what was found is gone,
and from the center moves the sun,
till love and loss are one.

Catskill Winter Storm

To remember Marilyn Russell

The pale sun seeps through bursts of rain and snow,
But the cold wind howls. It takes form, prowls the valleys
And the old mountains, bending birches, oaks, pines and balsams
To its whim. Not a bird takes to the rough air, nor a stray insect
flies.

The air, left to its own devices, flies into things, houses,
Slamming doors. Everything solid bends to the gale,
Holding on. The weak sun gives no comfort. Old bears make their
beds.
It is the seasonal killing time. Winter does its necessary work.

Inside a house a death is announced: Winter has taken
Its sacrifice, someone willing to go so that the others can live.
She had forgotten her name, so the wind swept her up in its arms
Without calling her. Her breath, stopping, became a part of the air

We breathe. In the failing light, in the storm,
We knew the absence; we breathed in to let her go.

The Naturalist

Nothing of him that doth fade
But doth suffer a sea-change
Into something rich and strange
—William Shakespeare, The Tempest

Within its box his squat pen is laid
never to turn again the earth
of our imaginings. The soil will
lie unlined and we are paid.
Don't be afraid.

When the troubles spilled and cracked his land,
he wrote for all, but some called him coward.
Where he saw the boys fall in the street,
he read "paras thirteen, bogside nil."
Now the lines have faded on the walls
but in his verse they stay,
and in that street boys play at games.
Don't be afraid.

He wrote to undeceive the world,
and when he raised his glass in Boston to his crowd
he asked: Where is the source of our suffering?
Do we hesitate to speak? *Don't be afraid.*
And then he laughed: Eat your good lamb.

The line spins out, his kite rises high and far
as waves rush on the beach and the sun shines fire,
the heat rises, the line melts and falls,
the kite flies off, itself alone, a shining pyre,
toward the future.
Don't be afraid.

Leakage

The drip, drip, drip of time
fell on crow
fell on fox
fell on bones
fell on stones over graves
fell on hands turning each hour
fell on young
fell on old, wrinkling flesh

Seconds fell into pools of minutes
Collecting into hours and days
Drowning each river-victim
Gurgling as they struggled
Sticks netting their escape

It fell on me

Place a coin in my mouth
That I may pass
To the land of no time.

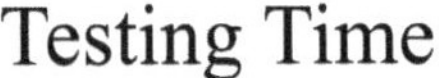

Testing Time

A Limited Bestiary

A wise old owl sat on an oak;
The more he saw the less he spoke;
The less he spoke the more he heard;
Why aren't we like that wise old bird?
—Nursery Rhyme

A famished owl was set to swing
Down on his latest offerings,
The more he heard the less he said,
The more he saw, the sooner fed.

The owl spied in the field below
Little marks on fallen snow
And heard the squeaks of ready meat.
Where he looked for his next treat.

And then his great white wings spread wide
Silence over countryside
Until he fell upon his prey—
A mouse of little pedigree.

Aren't we like that wise old bird?
Spotting targets seen or heard
Ripping victims with our law:
Wise owl, red in tooth and claw.

Original Sin: The Wound

Under the decks, in the galleys, rides
our nation's dark cargo, our illicit trade.
Like a spreading wound, it festers below.

Here's the orange menace, the grand puppeteer,
he points: *the ten thick worms his fingers.**
Like *the brazen giant of Greek fame**,* like the one-eyed,
the Washington mountaineer, who chuckles,
throw them in rough, don't be nice.
We all know to whom he points with his thick fingers—

Them, the other, the rainbow of colors,
the poor, the wretched refuse, the huddled masses.
Lock 'em up! Send 'em home back where they came from!
Build a beautiful wall, better than Berlin's,
the whole nation a prison.

Hey, wait: *We didn't land on Plymouth Rock,* said Malcolm X.
It landed on us. He said: *"There is a racist cancer, malignant,*
In the body of America."
The worms chew through our body politic.

In the cave with a Cyclopes, the one-eyed,
who will sharpen our spears?
US(A), US(A), US(A)!

Slavery has a long half-life.

We still ride that railroad,
underground. On the surface,
where politicians live
there is no sign of discontent, or shadows
to ruffle their smiles.

We cannot live half-slave, half free.
So we are all slaves now, underground, underwater,
galley slaves, rowing our captains and their kin
to their white mansions on the edge of wine-dark seas.

Slavery is America's wound.

*Osip Mandelstam, "The Stalin Epigram"
**Emma Lazarus, "The New Colossus"

Visa Number 457

The American Attaché in Berlin,
neatly dressed in suit and tie, said:
    Perhaps only 300 visas will be issued over the next few months,
    sorry about that.
The two with their ragged stars asked:
    Could we come back?
    We could bring something.

    Certainly, he said, smiling.
    You are cultured people.

My grandparents
were number
457 on the list
of the American Embassy
in Berlin
for a visa to
the United States.

They returned with a family jewel—
a black opal ring with blood-red highlights—and a note
that a very nice Persian rug would be delivered to his home.

    Well, he said, smiling, *if you go to the*
    Visa Office downstairs, you will be pleasantly surprised.

They were issued visa number 242.
In a month, they left for England
and then America.

Many years later, the German government
invited back a group of survivors whose property they had stolen.
On the plane, next to my aunt, sat another woman
perhaps the same age. They spoke for hours.

She told my aunt that her parents were lost, taken away
in cattle cars and were never heard from again. *They tried to leave*
but their visa was downgraded—we never knew why—
and they never made it
out.

Kristallnacht

In memory of my grandmother, Lilli Bing

Late that night in bed, we hear the window shatter.
The Nurnberg boys throw stones at the stained glass.
My husband rises—I say, no matter,
but for those with yellow stars it will not pass.

The Nurnberg boys throw stones. I sang
Bach, and Schiller's *Ode to Joy* in the Ninth,
before my voice was stopped by *sturm und drang.*
My mind was unprepared. It was the twenty-ninth

year I had sung Bach with the choir. And now, no more.
The Director's wife cried: *You must resign!* No ode to joy.
My mind was unprepared. Since then, blow on blow.
The *Sturmabteilung* comes at 3AM. Over there in blood lies a boy.

The Director's wife cries again, with tears, we both hear
the percussion while the voices fail. The SA
comes at 3AM; I remember nothing but fear.
Over Europe, I hear explosions, cries, and sirens wail.

All is percussion while the voices fail.
My husband wakes to his life, in tatters.
Across Europe I hear explosions and sirens wail.
Over and over we hear the windows shatter.

Has the circus come to town?

                                                There they are.
All these magicians, jugglers, barkers, freaks,
with pancake makeup. They look real enough,
parading through the town, led by the clowns.

They smile from every compass point,
in every bar, in clubs, an array of pixels.
They're in every home at night, flickering.
In the paper they're above the fold. Phone rings, it's them.

How strange they appear. They never make
mistakes. They have perfect teeth, perfect skin,
perfect smiles. They look like gods. And they make
you feel, well, less. As if you needed *them.*

I suppose it's OK if you like magic and such.
I asked how they do their tricks—went to shake
a hand, but—I grasped air and he faded
away. He had already made his trick.

There was the ticket to ride, then three-card monte
(lost some money there, of course), then a stage
act with cannons and gunfire everywhere,
even knocked down a building with people in it.

My wife and I, we're leaving. We're going to light out
for the territory. Had a friend once, he did that,
went away after he told me he wasn't going to stand
for more civilizing. He didn't want to be perfect, I guess.

Sad to leave our neighbors, but they've changed.
They love the magicians. They believe what they hear.

They do what they're told.

Lamentation on the Ruin of the Polity

After A. E. Housman's "Epitaph on an Army of Mercenaries"

These, in the days when the swamp is rising,
The time some say is near end-time,
Follow their mercenary calling
And take their plunder amid the slime.

Our leaders fail to hold the earth
Intact. It fractures in their arms.
What evil slouches now to birth
No one yet knows.
                    Sound alarms.

Reading Hart Crane

Reading Crane, his ecstatic homage
to a bridge and to his life,
I find marks next to the print,
made in pencil, marks by someone
who had read the poem before, long ago.

The marks seem made for me, perhaps,
offer friendly guidance, perhaps.
They point the way, next to a line here or there.

I realize suddenly that they are my own.

Where was I then, where am I now,
in this great mysterious sea?
How strange to find, in bottle or book,
A message from myself.

A bedlamite from the parapet,
Or a writer,
Or just an old man,
To whom did this young man write his messages?

Reading Crane, I see my younger self.

I read my own telltales
                                        too late to change.

Family Time

Allen Oldfather Whipple

A daguerreotype from 1884 shows Allen and three other
small ones on a donkey, posed in amber in the shutter's oval.
On bleak Mt. Sier, in Urmiah, Persia,

a sister and two brothers—Mildred, Maxwell, and Willie,
lie in the missionary graveyard under small crosses.
Allen and two others lived and returned,

he with six languages and determination. First a doctor,
then a surgeon, then a teacher, then a scholar. My grandfather
taught me chess, charity, and kindness,

with humility I have yet to learn. He taught surgeons their craft,
wrote how medicine emerged from the Greeks
and traveled, through Arabs and Assyrians, to the Renaissance.

I have the inlaid chess table he made,
the dining table pegged from the boards of a farm fence.
In one photo, he wears a cravat and round eyeglasses.

Bottles were his curse: His wife, son and daughter,
all lived near the bottle. He, missionaries' son,
did not judge. He loved them each and all.

After his beloved wife Mary had gone
his son returned with his bottles and pain.
His father loved him to the end.

Near his end, Allen returned to Persia to teach surgeons
and to Mt. Seir to visit his family, under the crosses.

After he died, relatives ransacked his small apartment.

Alpine Calendars

My father told me of the alpine mountains he climbed when young. I saw them from a distance, on calendars, each year presenting twelve new mountains. The snow never left the peaks, and the shadows of clouds fell on the valleys.

Once my father and I climbed a mountain in Colorado and on the way met a solitary climber who said that all sensations originate in feet. A crazy, said my father. Then my father showed me how to slide down a glacier using a stick for a brake. Climbing later only with my father's memories, I remember his mountains. Those are the ones I climb, even if he had never seen them. I linger at the top, waiting for the late afternoon storms to hasten my return.

Climbing through time, I view
the past in the valleys
through the mists below.

The Concert Grand

The immigrant spoke of the value of the things
his parents and grandparents brought from Europe
at expense, at risk, desperate refugees.

Armoires, tables, paintings, chairs in the Louis Quatorze style,
Etruscan vases, funereal statues in glass cages—
and the concert grand piano floated to the shores of the new world.

He saved what he could from the cauldron of Europe,
each still warm from the fires.
What remained was what remained of their lost world.

In the new world there was nothing old,
all was new and modern and white or pink or black,
either oven-hot or refrigerator-cold.

All that is modern is real and useful, and already here,
but the tide brought in the old
and flung them on our plastic shores.

The stories came with the tide, flowing from
the immigrant's voice, connecting family and memory
to places and times of both champagne and misery.

The stories were the soul of every object.
The stories burnished their old world splendors—
How the tables held gold-rimmed plates, and the chairs
    noble rumps,

and the music, Schubert and Mozart and Brahms,
was played by the immigrant himself on the great black
    Bosendorfer,
in the new world as in the old.

The immigrant died. The armoires emptied,
and the paintings faded.
None knew their provenance.

The calendars displayed photographs of the Matterhorn,
the Jungfrau, and the Lauterbrunnen valley,
But the dates were all wrong.

All the objects became valueless, without souls.
Old letters from the famous
faded to blank papers, drifting away.

The books, in foreign languages, now unreadable,
went off to second-hand shops
for a proper burial. The silver was melted.

When the immigrant died, the concert grand fell silent,
its spirit alienated, the great sounding board
sounding no more.

We, survivors, opened and closed our white refrigerators,
cooked our meals on spotless black stoves,
chewed our frozen food in soundless halls.

Tides

We live at the margins of the ocean now.
We gather the largesse of the sea.
We live at the whim of the moon,
dragging the water near and then away.
We wait for the big tide, the rising water,
when the sun and the moon will pull together,
catch us, and drag us out.

Till then we are each other's refuge,
too old to be compared to flowers or
spring's lush life, fragrant colors or
its succulence, its freshness, its promise.

Instead we prize touch,
which, although it does not inflame,
yields a buoyancy that lifts us,
wrinkled by our long floating,
above the rising waters until
the tide takes us out.

Two Gardeners

Annihilating all that's made
To a green thought in a green shade.
—Andrew Marvell, "The Garden"

In spring, he digs and culls rocks
preparing soil for seeds.

The green snake curves over the earth
frightening the gardener from her innocent labors.

The cold Chablis they drink on a hot summer's day
retains a taste of the earth. The apple is tart.

The garden riots in the summer, discovering all colors
which, in the fall, dry to brown.

Her curved back fits his body, and grows warmer;
Thus rooted, they blossom, then grow old.

In winter, there is no garden. Just plots
without markers, where all the other seasons lie buried.

Traveling West at Altitude

For Cass

Traveling west at altitude, in late day,
when the country below slowly darkens
and the serpentine rivers run unhurriedly past
towns gradually returning home,

when the stringed lights come on,
and the world is altogether innocent,
without a hint of politics, discord, or even hope.
It is simply evening.

Now the sun slows its descent
the red rim of earth radiates light
and the sun shimmers. Time itself
slows, and I think well, aren't you my sun,

which colors the sky and makes each minute
extend itself in calm and peaceful serenity,
lighting the remaining evening
with a constant fire which, gently,

darkens into lateness.
This you have given me:
The shimmer at the end of the day,
this light before dark.

Unmaking

There are so many things that deserve unmaking.
Traffic jams, floods and taking friends for granted.
Some marriages, when there is no giving, only taking.

Many homes, after long leave-taking
come apart at the seams, and, floors slanted,
become ruined reminders, painted walls flaking.

Pestilence and the virus of politics—
a disordered season and the sound of rants,
and the not too distant cracks of democracy breaking.

Why, the whole nation requires unmaking
from the corruption and the fear of others and chants
which define us. We weary of giving while others are taking.

Wars deserve their own stanza of unmaking
from those who profit from horror and give scant
hope to the those who suffer from their taking.

And I myself, tottering, overstaying and quaking,
settling to the earth, my final berth, I can't
stay perpendicular, am almost breaking—
even I—*say* it!—deserve unmaking.

Desert Time

Juniper Bush

This one juniper bush
rooted solitary in the desert
home to a flock of bluebirds last week

now swings its limbs excitedly
in the whirling desert gusts
like Vishnu as Bernstein

conducting the wild symphony of the winds.

The Adobe Builder

He takes a stick and draws a line in sand
that makes a curve in the earth, a delicate arc,
the shaping of a wall.

Then comes the trench, with cinder blocks inside,
concrete flowing to the brim. Next are placed
sun-dried bricks of earth.

His hands begin to shape the mud that binds
the bricks. Mud against mud, flesh against earth,
the ancient link again.

The wall goes up, brick by brick until
it reaches the desired height. The builder
rests with tired pride.

The curves he scratched into the sand back then
have grown into a set of arcs that flow
across the unmarked desert.

Around the house is now a graceful wall,
grown from the earth itself into itself,
its very nature shaped.

What is the builder but a man who makes
a frame that curves and shapes the lives of all
contained within that frame?

Seasons of the Desert in New Mexico

The dust. The sand. The ants, their nests, hills built
grain by grain. And over dust and sand,
black ravens fly.

Fall

First two coyotes slink across the road
drinking from the birdbath. Then paired towhees
peck upon the ground, one feeding the other,
beak to beak, then drink from an over-
flowing pot. In evening, a third coyote
forages under the feeder. All are released
by the cooling wind blowing dusk to the desert.
Ravens perch.

Winter

Water freezes in the birdbaths and water barrels,
the ice, the cold, the sand, life that yields,
its time yet to come.

Spring

The little rain that falls wets hidden seeds.
From dirt, from sand, from hills of sand come
green tendrils, breaking the hard ground. Ravens peck
at the earth while drying their wings.

Summer

The dust, the sand, the ants—and then the flowers
break out to challenge the monochrome, in blue
and red, orange and yellow and green. Thunder
announces the monsoon and horsetails of rain rivulet

down into arroyos that grow into streams that dig
into the sand and cut channels. Animals flee
to higher ground as rain and flares and thunder
give life again.

The drying sun returns the round again,
the dust, the sand, the ants rebuild their mounds,
and over dust and sand, black ravens fly.

The Beauty of Ordinary Things

This spoon, this plate, this blue bowl of dark-red cherries
This mug, spreading through the air the smell of strong coffee
This cupboard filled with heavy and simple brown plates
This window, through which the yellow and ochre desert appears
This room, where the food that nourishes and sustains is prepared.

This house of rooms, each with its own purpose
This house in the desert, cool in summer, warm in winter
These plots, with homes of neighbors, who came for beauty and
    peace
And found it, mostly. These mountains, eternal and unyielding.

The winds that flow about the mountains to the desert below,
These days that move in an eternal circle toward each one's end
These months and years that have no end until they do.

Time, first at our backs and then in our faces,
Moves through lives as wind stirs sand.

But always, this bright blue bowl of dark-red cherries.

Aquarius' Blessing

The world begins at sunrise in the desert,
with the squawking of a raven, the distant
coyotes' yowl.

Sunrise is as sunset, brilliant, colorful.
Bluebirds flock in juniper bushes—
turquoise glints.

The wind gathers, at first gentle, rustling yucca spines,
but the afternoon brings waves of heat and a
scorching howl.

Every living thing, from cholla to lizards to
blue flax flowers, await the monsoon,
Aquarius' blessing.

And when at last the sky turns to gray
and water horsetails down in sheets
the arroyos run.

Permissions

About the Author

John Bing has spent some of his lifetime building metaphorical bridges, but most of his time amazed at and appreciating different cultures and peoples, from a number of countries in Africa and Europe and Latin America to his years—years ago—in Afghanistan as a Peace Corps Volunteer. From these wanderings, and now from his perch in the American southwest, he has come to love both the peoples he has met and the lands that they inhabit. Just as each person and each group have their own characteristics and belief systems, so every place has its particular geography and set of living things.

His poetry works at distilling these differences and similarities into their essences.

www.ingramcontent.com/pod-product-compliance
Lightning Source LLC
LaVergne TN
LVHW041929090826
845145LV00017B/2703

9781954353008